Presented To:

Presented By:

Date:

GOD'S LITTLE INSTRUCTION BOOK

Honor Books

Tulsa, Oklahoma

God's Little Instruction Book
ISBN 1-56292-859-7
Copyright © 2000 by Honor Books
P. O. Box 55388
Tulsa, Oklahoma 74155

Introduction

God's Little Instruction Book is an inspirational collection of quotes and scriptures that will motivate you to live a meaningful, productive, and happy life. Some books contain quotes and others have scriptures, but this one offers both: insight from humanity's best minds and the wisdom of the ages: God's Word.

Positive, practical, and filled with the Bible's timeless wisdom, this delightful book offers a road map to succeed in the daily journey of life. We at Honor Books hope you will learn to treasure *God's Little Instruction Book* as much as we do.

A marriage may be made in heaven, but the maintenance must be done on earth.

Nevertheless let every one of you in particular so love his wife even as himself; and the wife see that she reverence her husband.

EPHESIANS 5:33

When God measures a man,
He puts the tape around the
heart instead of the head.

The LORD seeth not as man seeth; for man looketh on the outward appearance, but the LORD looketh on the heart.

1 SAMUEL 16:7

*T*he grass may look greener on the other side, but it still has to be mowed.

Be content with such things as ye have.

HEBREWS 13:5

*P*atience is the ability to keep your motor idling when you feel like stripping your gears.

He that is slow to anger is better than the mighty; and he that ruleth his spirit than he that taketh a city.

PROVERBS 16:32

$\mathcal{H}$e who is waiting for something to turn up might start with his own shirt sleeves.

All hard work brings a profit,
but mere talk leads only to poverty.

PROVERBS 14:23 NIV

*R*emember the banana—
when it left the bunch,
it got skinned.

Not forsaking the assembling of ourselves together, as the manner of some is; but exhorting one another: and so much the more, as ye see the day approaching.

HEBREWS 10:25

*I*t is better to be silent and be considered a fool than to speak and remove all doubt.

Yea also, when he that is a fool walketh by the way, his wisdom faileth him, and he saith to every one that he is a fool.

ECCLESIASTES 10:3

*M*any a good man has failed because he had his wishbone where his backbone should have been.

Have not I commanded thee? Be strong and of a good courage; be not afraid, neither be thou dismayed: for the LORD thy God is with thee whithersoever thou goest.

JOSHUA 1:9

*I*f at first you don't
succeed, try reading
the instructions.

Take fast hold of instruction; let her not go:
keep her; for she is thy life.

PROVERBS 4:13

*Y*our temper is like a fire.
It gets very destructive
when it gets out of control.

He that hath no rule over his own spirit is like a city
that is broken down, and without walls.

PROVERBS 25:28

*D*ecisions can take you out
of God's will but never
out of His reach.

If we are faithless, he will remain faithful,
for he cannot disown himself.

2 TIMOTHY 2:13 NIV

*Y*our companions are like the buttons on an elevator. They will either take you up or they will take you down.

He that walketh with wise men shall be wise:
but a companion of fools shall be destroyed.

PROVERBS 13:20

*P*atience is a quality you admire
in the driver behind you and
scorn in the one ahead.

*The end of a matter is better than its beginning, and patience
is better than pride. Do not be quickly provoked in
your spirit, for anger resides in the lap of fools.*

ECCLESIASTES 7:8-9 NIV

*T*here is a name for people who
are not excited about
their work—unemployed.

Whatsoever ye do, do it heartily,
as to the Lord, and not unto men.

COLOSSIANS 3:23

A person's true character is revealed
by what he does
when no one is watching.

*Obey them not only to win their favor when their eye is on you,
but like slaves of Christ, doing the will of God from your heart.*

EPHESIANS 6:6 NIV

It's better to die with a good
name than to
live with a bad one.

A good name is better than precious ointment.

ECCLESIASTES 7:1

" *No*" is one of the few words that can never be misunderstood.

Let your statement be "Yes, yes" or "No, no."

MATTHEW 5:37 NASB

Too many churchgoers are singing "Standing on the Promises" when all they are doing is sitting on the premises.

That ye be not slothful, but followers of them who through faith and patience inherit the promises.

HEBREWS 6:12

*S*ome people complain because God put thorns on roses, while others praise Him for putting roses among thorns.

Finally, brethren, whatsoever things are true, whatsoever things are honest, whatsoever things are just, whatsoever things are pure, whatsoever things are lovely, whatsoever things are of good report; if there be any virtue, and if there be any praise, think on these things.

PHILIPPIANS 4:8

*T*he cure of crime is not in
the electric chair,
but in the high chair.

Train up a child in the way he should go:
and when he is old, he will not depart from it.

PROVERBS 22:6

The bridge you burn now may
be the one you later
have to cross.

If it be possible, as much as lieth in you,
live peaceably with all men.

ROMANS 12:18

The measure of a man is not
how great his faith is but
how great his love is.

And now these three remain: faith, hope and love.

But the greatest of these is love.

1 CORINTHIANS 13:13 NIV

$\mathcal{R}$eal friends are those who, when you've made a fool of yourself, don't feel you've done a permanent job.

Beareth all things, believeth all things, hopeth all things, endureth all things. Charity never faileth.

1 CORINTHIANS 13:7-8

*B*e careful that your marriage doesn't become a duel instead of a duet.

Let us therefore follow after the things which make for peace, and things wherewith one may edify another.

ROMANS 14:19

*T*he mighty oak was once a
little nut that stood
its ground.

*A man shall not be established by wickedness: but the root
of the righteous shall not be moved.*

PROVERBS 12:3

*T*he secret of achievement is to
not let what you're doing
get to you before you get to it.

*Commit thy works unto the LORD, and thy
thoughts shall be established.*

PROVERBS 16:3

*M*ost people wish to serve
God—but only in an
advisory capacity.

Humble yourselves therefore under the mighty hand of God,
that he may exalt you in due time.

1 PETER 5:6

Conscience is God's built-in warning system. Be very happy when it hurts you. Be very worried when it doesn't.

And herein do I exercise myself, to have always a conscience void to offense toward God, and toward men.

ACTS 24:16

*M*ost men forget God all day
and ask Him to remember
them at night.

Evening, and morning, and at noon, will I pray,
and cry aloud: and he shall hear my voice.

PSALM 55:17

If you don't stand for
something you'll fall
for anything!

If you do not stand firm in your faith,
you will not stand at all.

ISAIAH 7:9 NIV

*T*he measure of a man's character is not what he gets from his ancestors, but what he leaves his descendants.

A good man leaveth an inheritance to his children's children:
and the wealth of the sinner is laid up for the just.

PROVERBS 13:22

Although the tongue weighs very little, few people are able to hold it.

Even so the tongue is a little member, and boasteth great things.
Behold, how great a matter a little fire kindleth!

JAMES 3:5

*Y*ou should never let
adversity get you down—
except on your knees.

Is any one of you in trouble? He should pray.

JAMES 5:13 NIV

*H*e who wants milk should not
sit on a stool in the middle of
the pasture expecting the
cow to back up to him.

He becometh poor that dealeth with a slack hand:
but the hand of the diligent maketh rich.

PROVERBS 10:4

*T*he best bridge between hope and despair is often a good night's sleep.

It is vain for you to rise up early, to sit up late, to eat the bread
of sorrows: for so he giveth his beloved sleep.

PSALM 127:2

It is good to remember that the tea kettle, although up to its neck in hot water, continues to sing.

Rejoice evermore. In every thing give thanks: for this is the will of God in Christ Jesus concerning you.

I THESSALONIANS 5:16,18

*I*t's good to be a Christian and know it, but it's better to be a Christian and show it!

By this shall all men know that ye are my disciples, if ye have love one to another.

JOHN 13:35

*S*orrow looks back.
Worry looks around.
Faith looks up.

Fixing our eyes on Jesus, the author and perfecter of faith, who for the joy set before Him endured the cross, despising the shame, and has sat down at the right hand of the throne of God.

HEBREWS 12:2 NASB

$\mathscr{A}$ man is never in worse company than when he flies into a rage and is beside himself.

He that is soon angry dealeth foolishly.

PROVERBS 14:17

*S*uccess in marriage is more than finding the right person. It's becoming the right person.

Thou, O man of God, flee these things; and follow after righteousness, godliness, faith, love, patience, meekness.

1 TIMOTHY 6:11

*F*ailure in people is caused more by
lack of determination than lack of talent.

Let us not be weary in well doing:
for in due season we shall reap, if we faint not.

GALATIANS 6:9

A man is rich according to what he is,
not according to what he has.

*There is that maketh himself rich, yet hath nothing: there is
that maketh himself poor, yet hath great riches.*

PROVERBS 13:7

*L*ife can only be understood by looking backward, but it must be lived by looking forward.

Jesus said unto him, No man, having put his hand to the plough, and looking back, is fit for the kingdom of God.

LUKE 9:62

*S*uccess comes in cans; failure comes in can'ts.

I can do all things through Christ which strengtheneth me.

PHILIPPIANS 4:13

*S*ometimes we are so busy adding
up our troubles that we forget
to count our blessings.

*I will remember the works of the LORD: surely I will remember thy wonders of
old. I will meditate also of all thy work, and talk of thy doings.*

PSALM 77:11-12

*F*alling down doesn't make you a failure, but staying down does.

A just man falleth seven times, and riseth up again.

PROVERBS 24:16

*I*f a task is once begun,
Never leave it 'till it's done.
Be the labor great or small,
Do it well or not at all.

I have glorified thee on the earth: I have finished
the work which thou gavest me to do.

JOHN 17:4

*T*ime is more valuable than money because time is irreplaceable.

Redeeming the time, because the days are evil.

EPHESIANS 5:16

The best way to forget your own problems is to help someone solve his.

Look not every man on his own things,
but every man also on the things of others.

PHILIPPIANS 2:4

*G*od can heal a broken heart,
but he has to have
all the pieces.

My son, give me thine heart.

PROVERBS 23:26

*A*uthority makes some people grow —and others just swell.

He that is greatest among you shall be your servant.
And whosoever shall exalt himself shall be abased;
and he that shall humble himself shall be exalted.

MATTHEW 23:11-12

*B*e more concerned with what
God thinks about you than what
people think about you.

Then Peter and the other apostles answered and said,
We ought to obey God rather than men.

ACTS 5:29

The trouble with the guy who talks too fast is that he often says something he hasn't thought of yet.

Be not rash with thy mouth, and let not thine heart be hasty
to utter anything before God: for God is in heaven,
and thou upon earth: therefore let thy words be few.

ECCLESIASTES 5:2

The best way to get the last word is to apologize.

If you have been trapped by what you said, ensnared by the words of your mouth, then do this, my son, to free yourself, since you have fallen into your neighbor's hands: Go and humble yourself; press your plea with your neighbor!

PROVERBS 6:2-3 NIV

*T*he train of failure
usually runs on the
track of laziness.

By much slothfulness the building decayeth; and through
idleness of the hands the house droppeth through.

ECCLESIASTES 10:18

A small house will hold
as much happiness
as a big one.

Better is a dish of vegetables where love is,
than a fattened ox served with hatred.

PROVERBS 15:17 NASB

When confronted with a Goliath-sized problem, which way do you respond: "He's too big to hit" or, like David, "He's too big to miss."

The LORD that delivered me out of the paw of the lion,
and out of the paw of the bear, he will deliver me
out of the hand of this Philistine.

I SAMUEL 17:37

*F*orget yourself for others and others will not forget you!

Therefore all things whatsoever ye would that men should do to you, do ye even so to them: for this is the law and the prophets.

MATTHEW 7:12

The secret of success is to start from scratch and keep on scratching.

The seed in the good soil, these are the ones who have heard the word in an honest and good heart, and hold it fast, and bear fruit with perseverance.

LUKE 8:15 NASB

*Y*ou will find the
key to success under
the alarm clock.

Love not sleep, lest thou come to poverty;
open thine eyes, and thou shalt be satisfied with bread.

PROVERBS 20:13

*T*he secret of contentment
is the realization that life
is a gift not a right.

But godliness with contentment is great gain. For we brought nothing into this world, and it is certain we can carry nothing out.

1 TIMOTHY 6:6-7

$\mathscr{T}$rue faith and courage
are like a kite—an opposing
wind raises it higher.

But they that wait upon the LORD shall renew their strength; they shall
mount up with wings as eagles; they shall run, and not be weary;
and they shall walk, and not faint.

ISAIAH 40:31

*I*n order to receive the direction from
God you must be able to receive
the correction from God.

My son, despise not thou the chastening of the Lord, nor faint when thou art
rebuked of him: For whom the Lord loveth he chasteneth,
and scourgeth every son whom he receiveth.

HEBREWS 12:5-6

*B*ury the hatchet, but not in someone's back.

When ye stand praying, forgive, if ye have ought against any: that your Father also which is in heaven may forgive you your trespasses.

MARK 11:25

*T*hose who bring sunshine to the lives
of others cannot keep it from themselves.

Be not deceived; God is not mocked:
for whatsoever a man soweth, that shall he also reap.

GALATIANS 6:7

*N*o man ever really finds out
what he believes in until he begins
to instruct his children.

Ye fathers, provoke not your children to wrath: but bring
them up in the nurture and admonition of the Lord.

EPHESIANS 6:4

Don't mistake activity for achievement. Busyness does not equal productiveness.

Martha was cumbered about much serving, and came to him, and said, Lord, dost thou not care that my sister hath left me to serve alone? Bid her therefore that she help me. And Jesus answered and said unto her, Martha, Martha, thou art careful and troubled about many things: But one thing is needful: and Mary hath chosen that good part, which shall not be taken away from her.

LUKE 10:40-42

It's the little things in life that determine the big things.

Thou hast been faithful over a few things, I will make thee ruler over many things: enter thou into the joy of thy lord.

MATTHEW 25:21

The doors of opportunity are marked "Push" and "Pull."

The soul of the sluggard desireth, and hath nothing:
but the soul of the diligent shall be made fat.

PROVERBS 13:4

You cannot win
if you do not begin.

Now therefore perform the doing of it; that as there was a
readiness to will, so there may be a performance
also out of that which ye have.

2 CORINTHIANS 8:11

*T*he best way to be
successful is to follow
the advice you give others.

He who ignores discipline despises himself,
but whoever heeds correction gains understanding.

PROVERBS 15:32 NIV

$\mathscr{C}$ontentment isn't getting what we
want but being satisfied
with what we have.

Not that I speak in respect of want: for I have learned,
in whatsoever state I am, therewith to be content.

PHILIPPIANS 4:11

*T*oo many people
quit looking for work
when they find a job.

He also that is slothful in his work
is brother to him that is a great waster.

PROVERBS 18:9

You can't take your money with you, but you can send it on ahead.

Lay not up for yourselves treasures upon earth, where moth and rust doth corrupt, and where thieves break through and steal: But lay up for yourselves treasures in heaven, where neither moth nor rust doth corrupt, and where thieves do not break through nor steal.

MATTHEW 6:19-20

*A*bility will enable a man to
go to the top, but it takes
character to keep him there.

The righteousness of the blameless makes a straight way for them,
but the wicked are brought down by their own wickedness.

PROVERBS 11:5 NIV

*Y*our words are
windows to your heart.

Out of the abundance of the heart the mouth speaketh.

MATTHEW 12:34

A shut mouth gathers no foot.

He that keepeth his mouth keepeth his life: but he that openeth wide his lips shall have destruction.

PROVERBS 13:3

*T*he only fool bigger than the person who knows it all is the person who argues with him.

He that reproveth a scorner getteth to himself shame: and
he that rebuketh a wicked man getteth himself a blot.

PROVERBS 9:7

A drowning man does not complain about the size of a life preserver.

Do all things without murmurings and disputings.

PHILIPPIANS 2:14

*B*lessed is he who, having nothing to say, refrains from giving wordy evidence of the fact.

The tongue of the wise useth knowledge aright:
but the mouth of fools poureth out foolishness.

PROVERBS 15:2

*L*uck: a loser's excuse
for a winner's position.

The soul of the sluggard desireth, and hath nothing:
but the soul of the diligent shall be made fat.

PROVERBS 13:4

*D*o the thing you fear and the
death of fear is certain.

Be strong and of a good courage, fear not, nor be afraid of them:
for the LORD thy God, he it is that doth go with thee;
he will not fail thee, nor forsake thee.

DEUTERONOMY 31:6

*G*od plus one
is always a majority!

If God be for us, who can be against us?

ROMANS 8:31

Whoever gossips to you will be a gossip of you.

*A talebearer revealeth secrets: but he that is of a
faithful spirit concealeth the matter.*

PROVERBS 11:13

*J*esus is a friend who
knows all your faults
and still loves you anyway.

But God commendeth his love toward us, in that,

while we were yet sinners, Christ died for us.

ROMANS 5:8

*I*gnorance is always
swift to speak.

Let every man be swift to hear, slow to speak, slow to wrath.

JAMES 1:19

*L*earn from other's mistakes rather
than making them all yourself.

The way of a fool is right in his own eyes:
but he that hearkeneth unto counsel is wise.

PROVERBS 12:15

*P*ick your friends
but not to pieces.

A man that beareth false witness against his neighbour
is a maul, and a sword, and a sharp arrow.

PROVERBS 25:18

*H*e who throws dirt loses ground.

Wherefore putting away lying, speak every man truth with his neighbour: for we are members one of another.

EPHESIANS 4:25

You don't have to lie
awake nights to succeed—
just stay awake days.

I must work the works of him that sent me, while it is day:

the night cometh, when no man can work.

JOHN 9:4

*T*he first step to wisdom
is silence; the second
is listening.

*A wise man will hear, and will increase learning; and a man of
understanding shall attain unto wise counsels.*

PROVERBS 1:5

*T*he greatest possession
you have is the twenty-four hours
directly in front of you.

There is a time there for every purpose and for every work.

ECCLESIASTES 3:17

The most valuable gift
you can give another is
a good example.

For I have given you an example,
that ye should do as I have done to you.

JOHN 13:15

*D*on't be afraid of pressure.
Remember that pressure is
what turns a lump of coal
into a diamond.

*Knowing this, that the trying of your faith worketh patience. But let patience
have her perfect work, that ye may be perfect and entire, wanting nothing.*

JAMES 1:3-4

A minute of thought is worth more than an hour of talk.

Set a watch, O LORD, before my mouth; keep the door of my lips.

PSALM 141:3

You can win
more friends with your ears
than with your mouth.

Let every man be swift to hear, slow to speak, slow to wrath.

JAMES 1:19

*I*t's not the outlook but the
uplook that counts.

Looking unto Jesus the author and finisher of our faith.

HEBREWS 12:2

*P*ut others before yourself,
and you can become
a leader among men.

But it shall not be so among you: but whosoever will be great
among you, let him be your minister; and whosoever
will be chief among you, let him be your servant.

MATTHEW 20:26-27

*F*eed your faith and your doubts will starve to death.

But we are not of those who shrink back to destruction,
but of those who have faith to the preserving of the soul.

HEBREWS 10:39 NASB

*N*ever pass up a chance
to keep your mouth shut.

Even a fool, when he holdeth his peace, is counted wise:
and he that shutteth his lips is esteemed a man of understanding.

PROVERBS 17:28

*I*t isn't hard to make a
mountain out of a molehill.
Just add a little dirt.

Starting a quarrel is like breaching a dam;
so drop the matter before a dispute breaks out.

PROVERBS 17:14 NIV

What counts is not the number of hours you put in, but how much you put in the hours.

Whatsoever thy hand findeth to do, do it with thy might.

ECCLESIASTES 9:10

*R*eputation is made
in a moment: character is
built in a lifetime.

My righteousness I hold fast, and will not let it go:
my heart shall not reproach me so long as I live.

JOB 27:6

*I*f you feel "dog tired" at night, maybe it's because you "growled" all day!

If it be possible, as much as lieth in you, live peaceably with all men.

ROMANS 12:18

*I*f you don't want the
fruits of sin, stay out of
the devil's orchard.

Abstain from all appearance of evil.

1 THESSALONIANS 5:22

*O*ur children are like mirrors—they reflect our attitudes in life.

The just man walketh in his integrity:
his children are blessed after him.

PROVERBS 20:7

The art of being a good
guest is knowing
when to leave.

Withdraw thy foot from thy neighbour's house;
lest he be weary of thee, and so hate thee.

PROVERBS 25:17

*H*e who cannot forgive
breaks the bridge over which
he himself must pass.

For if ye forgive men their trespasses,
your heavenly Father will also forgive you.

MATTHEW 6:14

*J*esus is a friend
who walks in when
the world has walked out.

These things I have spoken unto you, that in me ye might have peace.
In the world ye shall have tribulation: but be of good cheer;
I have overcome the world.

JOHN 16:33

*T*hose who deserve love
the least need it the most.

*I say unto you, Love your enemies, bless them that curse you,
do good to them that hate you, and pray for them which
despitefully use you, and persecute you.*

MATTHEW 5:44

*F*aith is daring the soul
to go beyond what
the eyes can see.

We walk by faith, not by sight.

2 CORINTHIANS 5:7

*T*he right angle to approach
a difficult problem is the
"try-angle."

With God nothing shall be impossible.

LUKE 1:37

*T*he fellow who does things
that count doesn't usually
stop to count them.

I can do all things through Christ which strengtheneth me.
Notwithstanding ye have well done,
that ye did communicate with my affliction.

PHILIPPIANS 4:13-14

A critical spirit is like poison ivy—
it only takes a little contact
to spread its poison.

*Avoid wordly and empty chatter, for it will lead to further
ungodliness, and their talk will spread like gangrene.*

2 TIMOTHY 2:16-17 NASB

Laziness and poverty are cousins.

A little sleep, a little slumber, a little folding of the hands to sleep:

So shall thy poverty come as one that travelleth;

and thy want as an armed man.

PROVERBS 24:33-34

*L*anguage is the expression
of thought. Every time you speak,
your mind is on parade.

A good man out of the good treasure of his heart bringeth forth
that which is good; and an evil man out of the evil treasure
of his heart bringeth forth that which is evil:
for of the abundance of the heart his mouth speaketh.

LUKE 6:45

*T*ake care of your character
and your reputation will
take care of itself.

*A good man leaveth an inheritance to his children's children:
and the wealth of the sinner is laid up for the just.*

PROVERBS 13:22

*T*he hardest secret
for a man to keep is
his opinion of himself.

I say, through the grace given unto me, to every man that is among you, not to think of himself more highly than he ought to think; but to think soberly, according as God hath dealt to every man the measure of faith.

ROMANS 12:3

He who buries his talent is
making a grave mistake.

Neglect not the gift that is in thee.

1 TIMOTHY 4:14

*I*f a care is too small to be turned into a prayer, it is too small to be made into a burden.

Casting all your care upon him; for he careth for you.

1 PETER 5:7

*E*ven a woodpecker owes his success to the fact that he uses his head.

But you, keep your head in all situations.

2 TIMOTHY 4:5 NIV

*T*he poorest of all men is not the man without a cent but the man without a dream.

Where there is no vision, the people perish.

PROVERBS 29:18

You can accomplish more in one hour with God than one lifetime without Him.

With God all things are possible.

MATTHEW 19:26

*T*he only preparation
for tomorrow is the
right use of today.

Take therefore no thought for the morrow: for the morrow shall take thought for the things of itself. Sufficient unto the day is the evil thereof.

MATTHEW 6:34

When things go wrong, don't go wrong with them.

Enter not into the path of the wicked,
and go not in the way of evil men.

PROVERBS 4:14

*T*wo things are hard on the heart—
running up stairs and
running down people.

Let no corrupt communication proceed out of your mouth, but that which is good to the use of edifying, that it may minister grace unto the hearers.

EPHESIANS 4:29

The best way to get even is to forget.

Love ye your enemies, and do good, and lend, hoping for nothing again;
and your reward shall be great, and ye shall be the children of
the Highest: for he is kind unto the unthankful and to the evil.

LUKE 6:35

*P*eople don't care how much
you know until they know
how much you care.

*Let nothing be done through strife or vainglory; but in lowliness of
mind let each esteem other better than themselves.*

PHILIPPIANS 2:3

*H*umor is to life what shock absorbers are to automobiles.

A merry heart doeth good like a medicine:
but a broken spirit drieth the bones.

PROVERBS 17:22

A man wrapped up
in himself makes a very
small package.

*A fool finds no pleasure in understanding but
delights in airing his own opinions.*

PROVERBS 18:2 NIV

It isn't your position that makes you happy or unhappy, it's your disposition.

But godliness with contentment is great gain. For we brought nothing into this world, and it is certain we can carry nothing out.

I TIMOTHY 6:6-7

*I*t takes more to plow a field
than merely turning it
over in your mind.

*Work with your hands, just as we commanded you, so that you
will behave properly toward outsiders and not be in any need.*

1 THESSALONIANS 4:11-12 NASB

*M*en are like fish.
Neither would get into trouble
if they kept their mouths shut.

Whoso keepeth his mouth and his tongue
keepeth his soul from troubles.

PROVERBS 21:23

The heart of a man cannot be determined by the size of his pocketbook.

What shall it profit a man, if he shall gain the whole world, and lose his own soul? Or what shall a man give in exchange for his soul?

MARK 8:36-37

*K*indness is the oil
that takes the
friction out of life.

But the fruit of the Spirit is . . . kindness.

GALATIANS 5:22 NIV

You can easily determine the caliber of a person by the amount of opposition it takes to discourage him.

If thou faint in the day of adversity, thy strength is small.

PROVERBS 24:10

*P*eople know what you are
by what they see, not by
what they hear.

*Let your light so shine before men, that they may see your
good works, and glorify your Father which is in heaven.*

MATTHEW 5:16

*P*eople who try to whittle you down
are only trying to
reduce you to their size.

Blessed are ye, when men shall hate you, and when they shall separate you
from their company, and shall reproach you, and cast out your
name as evil, for the Son of man's sake. Rejoice ye in that day, and
leap for joy: for, behold, your reward is great in heaven.

LUKE 6:22-23

Quite often when a man thinks his mind is getting broader, it's only his conscience stretching.

Unto the pure all things are pure: but unto them that are defiled and unbelieving is nothing pure; but even their mind and conscience is defiled.

TITUS 1:15

Temper is what gets most of us
into trouble. Pride is
what keeps us there.

Pride goeth before destruction, and an haughty spirit before a fall.
Better it is to be of an humble spirit with the lowly,
than to divide the spoil with the proud.

PROVERBS 16:18-19

We make a living by what we get—we make a life by what we give.

I have shewed you all things, how that so labouring ye ought to support the weak, and to remember the words of the Lord Jesus, how he said, It is more blessed to give than to receive.

ACTS 20:35

*O*ur days are identical suitcases—
all the same size—but some
people can pack more into
them than others.

Be very careful, then, how you live—not as unwise but as wise,
making the most of every opportunity.

EPHESIANS 5:15-16 NIV

*L*iving would be easier if
men showed as much patience
at home as they do when
they're fishing.

You husbands in the same way live with your wives in an understanding way.

1 PETER 3:7 NASB

*S*ome people succeed because they are destined to, but most people succeed because they are determined to.

Having done all, to stand. Stand therefore.

EPHESIANS 6:13-14

A man is rich according to what he is, not according to what he has.

There is that maketh himself rich, yet hath nothing: there is that maketh himself poor, yet hath great riches.

PROVERBS 13:7

*T*he difference between
ordinary and extraordinary
is that little extra.

Whatsoever thy hand findeth to do, do it with thy might; for there is no work,
nor device, nor knowledge, nor wisdom, in the grave, whither thou goest.

ECCLESIASTES 9:10

*S*wallowing angry words
is much better than
having to eat them.

*A fool uttereth all his mind: but a wise man
keepeth it in till afterwards.*

PROVERBS 29:11

*T*o forgive is to set a prisoner free and discover the prisoner was YOU.

If ye forgive men their trespasses, your heavenly Father will also forgive you: But if ye forgive not men their trespasses, neither will your Father forgive your trespasses.

MATTHEW 6:14-15

*T*he company you keep
will determine the
trouble you meet.

*Make no friendship with an angry man; and with a furious man thou
shalt not go: Lest thou learn his ways, and get a snare to thy soul.*

PROVERBS 22:24-25

*M*an cannot discover new oceans
unless he has the courage to
lose sight of the shore.

Peter answered him and said, Lord, if it be thou, bid me come
unto thee on the water. And he said, Come. And when Peter was
come down out of the ship, he walked on the water, to go to Jesus.

MATTHEW 14:28-29

*T*he heart is the happiest
when it beats for others.

Greater love hath no man than this, that a
man lay down his life for his friends.

JOHN 15:13

*O*ne thing you can learn by watching
the clock is that it passes time
by keeping its hands busy.

He also that is slothful in his work is brother

to him that is a great waster.

PROVERBS 18:9

*T*he best inheritance a father
can leave his children is
a good example.

*As ye know how we exhorted and comforted and charged
every one of you, as a father doth his children.*

1 THESSALONIANS 2:11

God intervenes in the affairs of men by invitation only.

Behold, I stand at the door, and knock: if any man hear my voice,
and open the door, I will come in to him, and will
sup with him, and he with me.

REVELATION 3:20

Additional Copies of this book and other titles
in the *God's Little Instruction Book* series
are available from your local bookstore.

God's Little Instruction Book for Men, leather edition
God's Little Instruction Book for Mom, leather edition
God's Little Instruction Book for Women, leather edition

If you have enjoyed this book, or if it has impacted your life,
we would like to hear from you. Please contact us at:

Honor Books
Department E
P. O. Box 55388
Tulsa, Oklahoma 74155

Or by e-mail at: info@honorbooks.com